Accent on MAJORS & Minors

by William Gillock

For Janet & Chris Mantooth

FOREWORD

Accent on Majors & Minors is a book with a purpose.

It is, first of all, a collection of literature for upper elementary/early intermediate level, and secondly, a theory workbook devoted to a better understanding of the keys and key signatures of the seven major and minor scales, which use as keynotes the seven white keys.

This presentation follows the recommended musicianship chart for Elementary C and D levels of the National Guild of Piano Teachers, and the pieces are of the required grade and length for auditions, as recommended in the suggested literature chart of this organization.

Accent on Majors & Minors is meant primarily as a basic study text for upper elementary grades, but it may also be used effectively as a corrective reading aid for intermediate-grade students where the deficiency is a lack of experience and/or knowledge of key variety.

William Gillock (1963)

CONTENTS

ISBN 978-1-4584-1158-7

EXCLUSIVELY DISTRIBUTED BY

HAL•LEONARD®
CORPORATION
7777 W. BLUEMOUND RD. P.O. BOX 13819
MILWAUKEE, WISCONSIN 53213

Visit Hal Leonard Online at
www.halleonard.com

PREPARATORY

What is the meaning of KEY ?

A family of related tones (scale) and chords which come to a <u>restful sound</u> on a specific tonality is called the "KEY OF — " in music. The <u>restful sounding</u> tone or chord gives the key its name. This tone or chord can be identified by the feeling <u>you</u> have of having "arrived home" after a musical journey. (Test yourself by playing a scale you know: which tone of the scale sounds like the "home tone?")

What is a SCALE ?

An orderly arrangement of tones whithin the compass of one octave is called a scale. There are many different kinds of scales. Here is one made entirely of half tones:

When you play this scale, notice that you do not skip a key in the entire octave. This is called the CHROMATIC SCALE because it uses all the tone colors known to the music of our Occidental culture.

Here is a scale made entirely of whole tones:

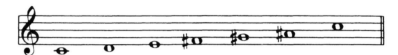

When you play this scale, notice that you <u>do</u> skip a key between each two tones. This is called the WHOLE TONE SCALE because all the tones are whole steps from each other.

The pieces in this book are written in the familiar Major and Minor keys which are based on the DIATONIC SCALE of seven tones — one tone for each letter name of the musical alphabet.

In the Major Scale half steps occur between the 3d-4th degrees and the 7th-8th:

In the Minor Scale half steps occur between the 2d-3d degrees and the 5th-6th. This arrangement produces the NATURAL MINOR SCALE, sometimes called the SIGNATURE MINOR:

A popular variation of this scale is the HARMONIC MINOR wherein the 7th tone of the natural minor scale is raised a half step by the use of an accidental:

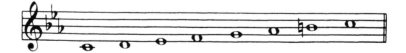

Another equally popular variation of the minor scale is the MELODIC MINOR wherein the 6th and 7th tones of the natural minor scale are raised a half step in ascending patterns and the natural minor scale is followed in descending patterns:

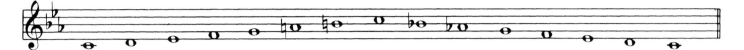

In the following pages minor scales are presented in their natural form. The author suggests that you practice the Harmonic and Melodic variations, also.

What are the CHORDS of a key?

Triads built on each degree of the scale are the chords of the key:

These chords and the tones of the scale are identified by Roman numerals, but they also have names: I- Tonic; II- Super Tonic; III- Mediant; IV- Sub Dominant; V- Dominant; VI- Sub Mediant; VII- Sub Tonic.

What is a CADENCE?

An arrangement of chords which comes to rest on the Tonic Chord is called a CADENCE.
Here is an easy way to form an authentic cadence which uses a I-IV-I-V-I sequence of chords:

What is a KEY SIGNATURE?

The sharps or flats (or absence of these) at the beginning of each staff is called KEY SIGNATURE. Since you will be asked to write the key signatures on the following pages, PLAY on the keyboard and MEMORIZE the order of sharps and flats:

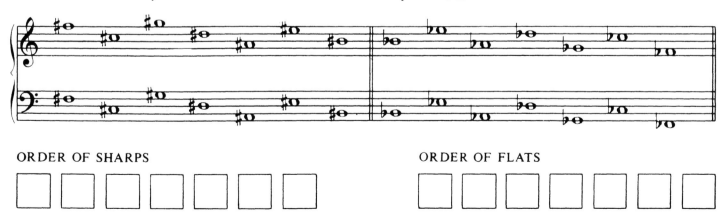

ORDER OF SHARPS

□ □ □ □ □ □ □

ORDER OF FLATS

□ □ □ □ □ □ □

KEY OF C MAJOR

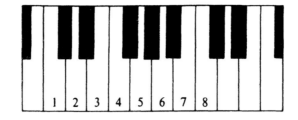

Write the names of the keys in the boxes

Here are the notes of the scale of C Major in 4 octaves, the 7 chords of the scale and the authentic cadence.

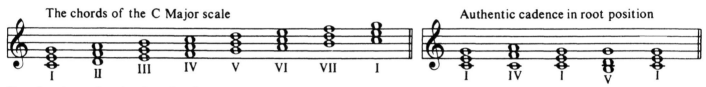

Practice the scale, chords and cadence as your teacher directs.

The following piece, SIDEWALK WALTZ, is written in the key of C Major.

SIDEWALK WALTZ

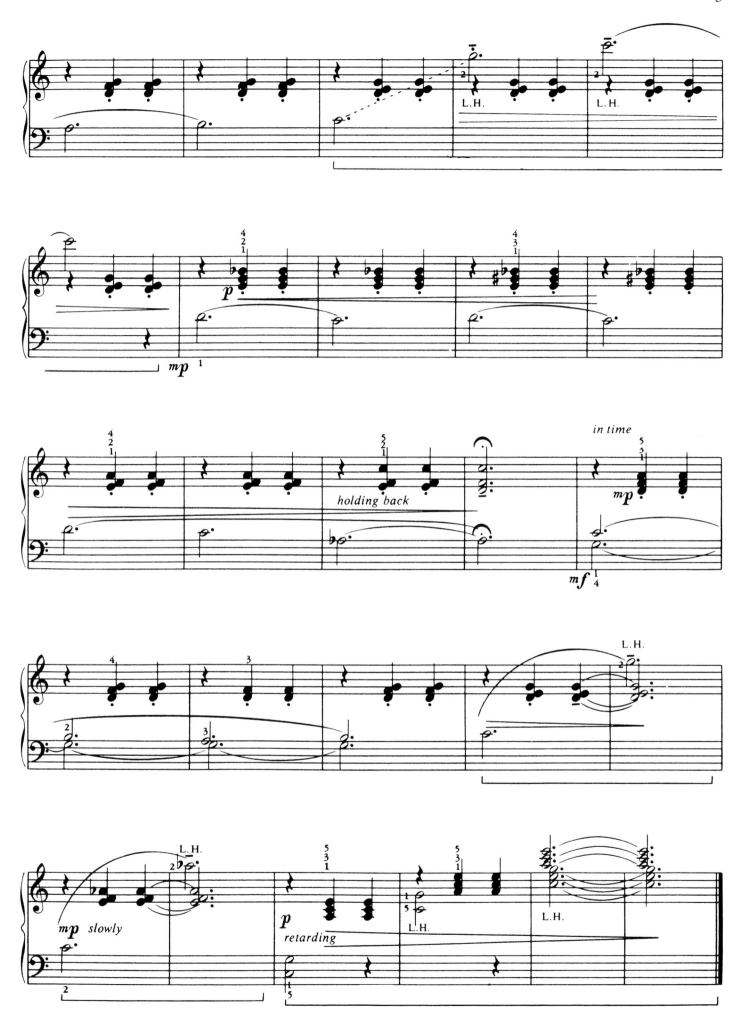

KEY OF C MINOR

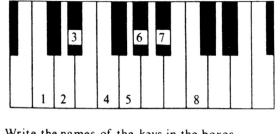

Write the names of the keys in the boxes

Here are the notes of the scale of C Minor in 4 octaves, the 7 chords of the scale and the authentic cadence. Write the key signature at the beginning of each staff, and fill in with pencil all the notes that will be played on black keys.

The chords of the C Minor scale

Authentic cadence in root position

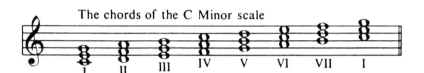
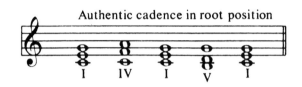

Practice the scale, chords and cadence as your teacher directs.

The following piece, WINDY WEATHER, is written in the key of C MINOR. Before you play it, write the key signature at the beginning of each staff.

WINDY WEATHER

KEY OF G MAJOR

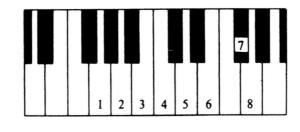

Write the names of the keys in the boxes

Here are notes of the scale of G Major in 4 octaves, the 7 chords of the scale and the authentic cadence. Write the key signature at the beginning of each staff, and fill in with pencil all of the notes that will be played on black keys.

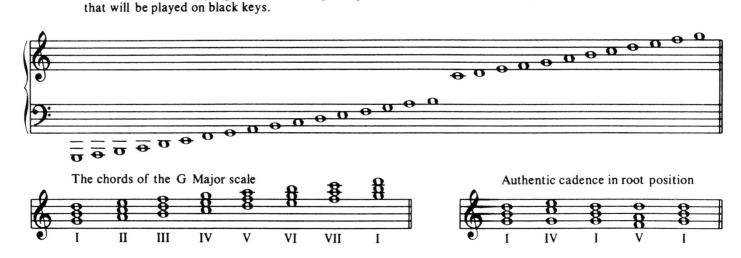

The chords of the G Major scale

I II III IV V VI VII I

Authentic cadence in root position

I IV I V I

Practice the scale, chords and cadence as your teacher directs.

The following piece, DANCING IN THE GARDEN, is written in the key of G Major. Before you play it, write the key signature at the beginning of each staff.

DANCING IN THE GARDEN

Moderately

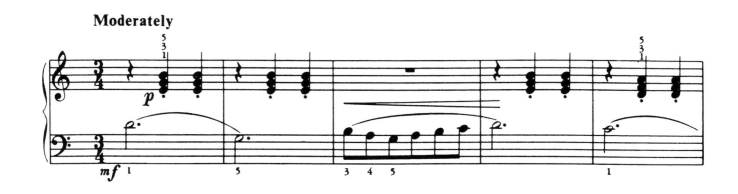

KEY OF G MINOR

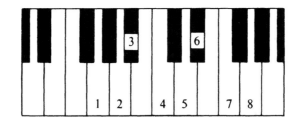

Write the names of the keys in the boxes

Here are the notes of the scale of G Minor in 4 octaves, the 7 chords of the scale and the authentic cadence. Write the key signature at the beginning of each staff, and fill in with pencil all the notes that will be played on black keys.

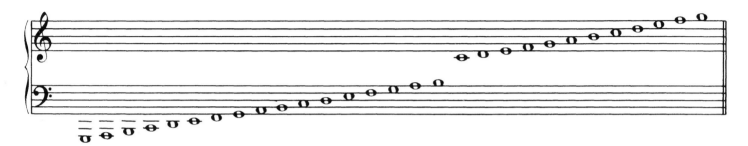

The chords of the G Minor scale.   Authentic cadence in root position

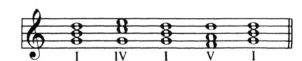

Practice the scale, chords and cadence as your teacher directs.

The following piece, DANCE IN ANCIENT STYLE, is written in the key of G Minor. Before you play it, write the key signature at the beginning of each staff.

DANCE IN ANCIENT STYLE

Decisively

KEY OF D MAJOR

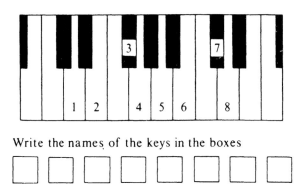

Write the names of the keys in the boxes

Here are the notes of the scale of D Major in 4 octaves, the 7 chords of the scale and the authentic cadence. Write the key signature at the beginning of each staff, and fill in with pencil all of the notes that will be played on black keys.

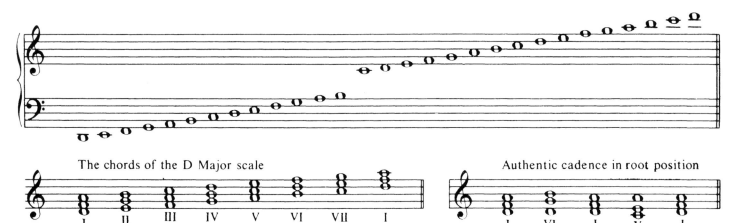

The chords of the D Major scale

I II III IV V VI VII I

Authentic cadence in root position

I VI I V I

Practice the scale, chords and cadence as your teacher directs.

The following piece, CARILLON, is written in the key of D Major. Before you play it, write the key signature at the beginning of each staff.

CARILLON

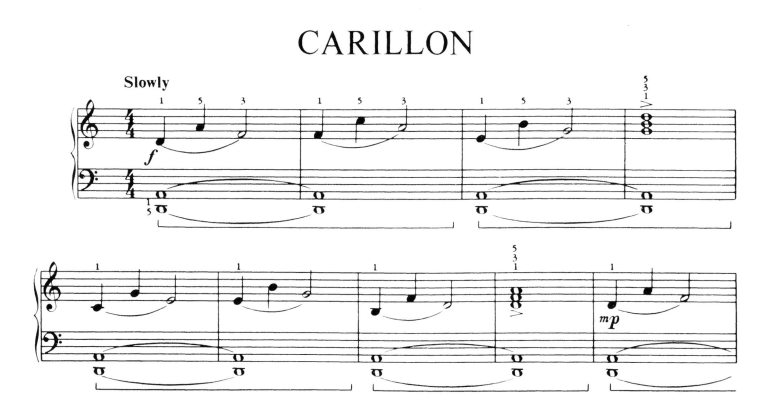

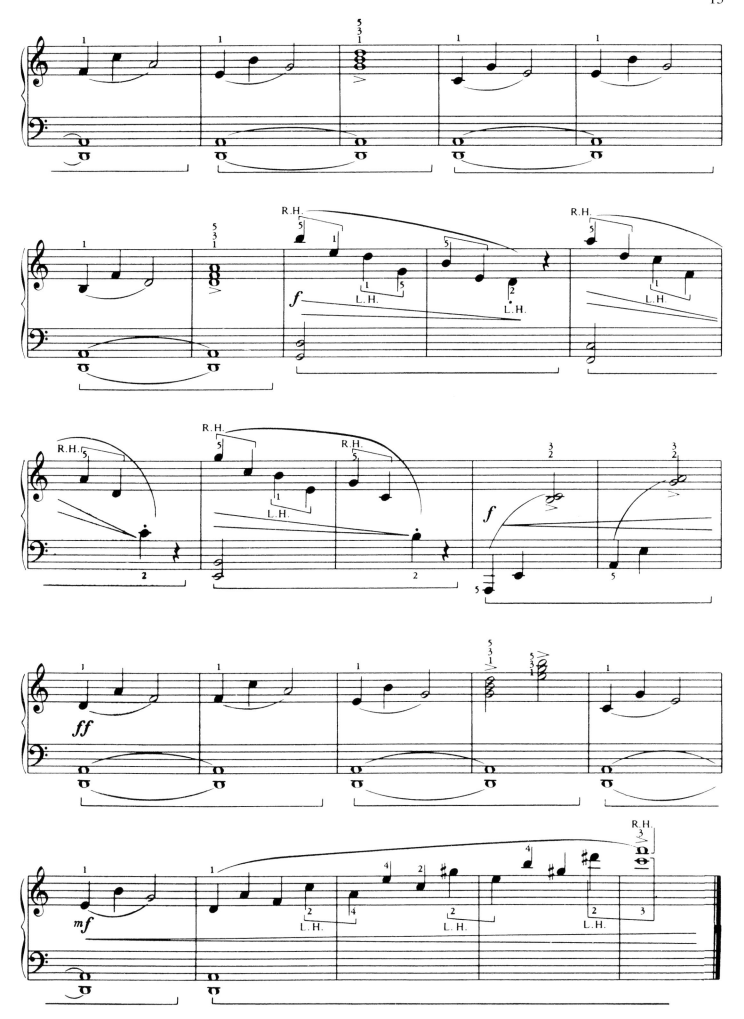

KEY OF D MINOR

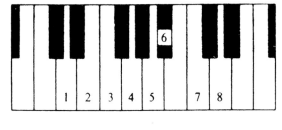

Write the names of the keys in the boxes

Here are the notes of the scale of D Minor in 4 octaves, the 7 chords of the scale and the authentic cadence. Write the key signature at the beginning of each staff, and fill in with pencil all of the notes that will be played on black keys.

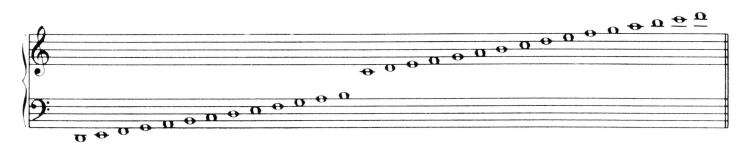

The chords of the D Minor scale

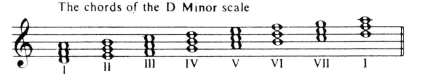

Authentic cadence in root position

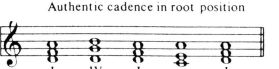

Practice the scale, chords and cadence as your teacher directs.

The following piece, **FLYING LEAVES**, is written in the key of D Minor. Before you play it, write the key signature at the beginning of each staff.

FLYING LEAVES

With smooth motion

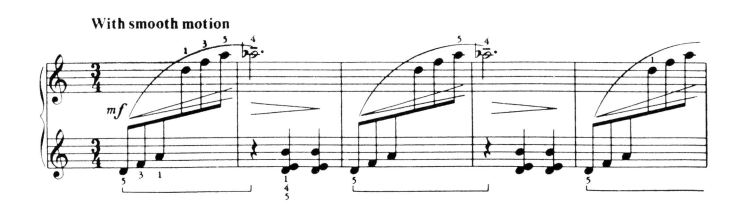

KEY OF A MAJOR

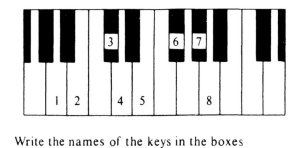

Write the names of the keys in the boxes

Here are the notes of the scale of A Major in 4 octaves, the 7 chords of the scale and the authentic cadence. Write the key signature at the beginning of each staff, and fill in with pencil all the notes that will be played on black keys.

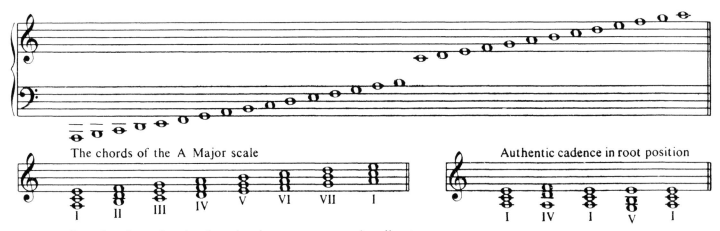

The chords of the A Major scale

Authentic cadence in root position

Practice the scale, chords and cadence as your teacher directs.

The following piece, WAGON TRAIN, is written in the key of A Major. Before you play it, write the key signature at the beginning of each staff.

WAGON TRAIN

Jauntily

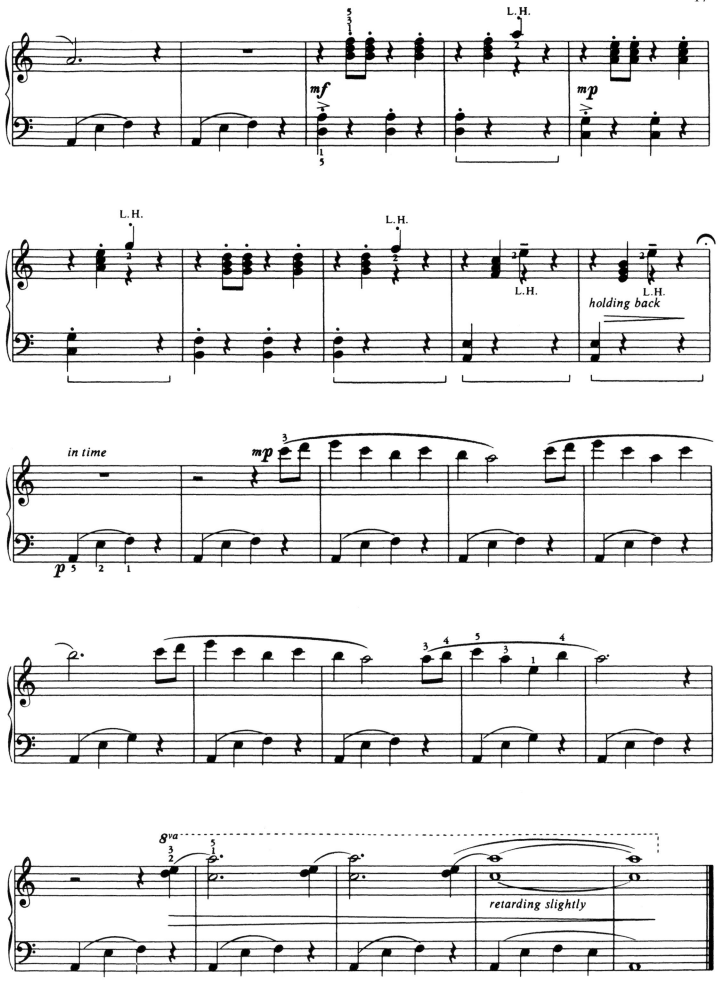

KEY OF A MINOR

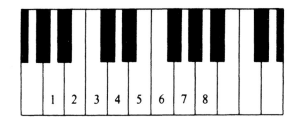

Write the names of the keys in the boxes

Here are the notes of the scale of A Minor in 4 octaves, the 7 chords of the scale and the authentic cadence.

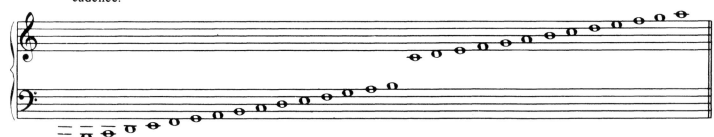

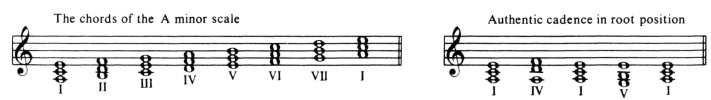

The chords of the A minor scale

Authentic cadence in root position

Practice the scale, chords and cadence as your teacher directs.

The following piece, MAZURKA, is written in the key of A Minor.

MAZURKA

Tempo di mazurka

KEY OF E MAJOR

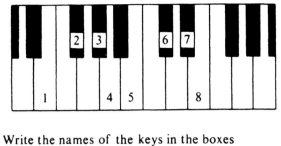

Write the names of the keys in the boxes

Here are the notes of the scale of E Major in 4 octaves, the 7 chords of the scale and the authentic cadence. Write the key signature at the beginning of each staff, and fill in with pencil all of the notes that will be played on black keys.

The chords of the E Major scale

I   II   III   IV   V   VI   VII   I

Authentic cadence in root position

I   IV   I   V   I

Practice the scale, chords and cadence as your teacher directs.

The following piece, SUMMERTIME CAPRICE, is written in the key of E Major. Before you play it, write the key signature at the beginning of each staff.

SUMMERTIME CAPRICE

In a flowing style

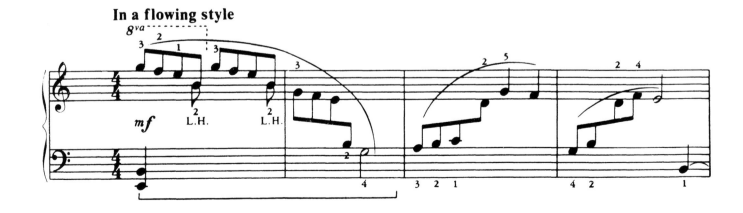

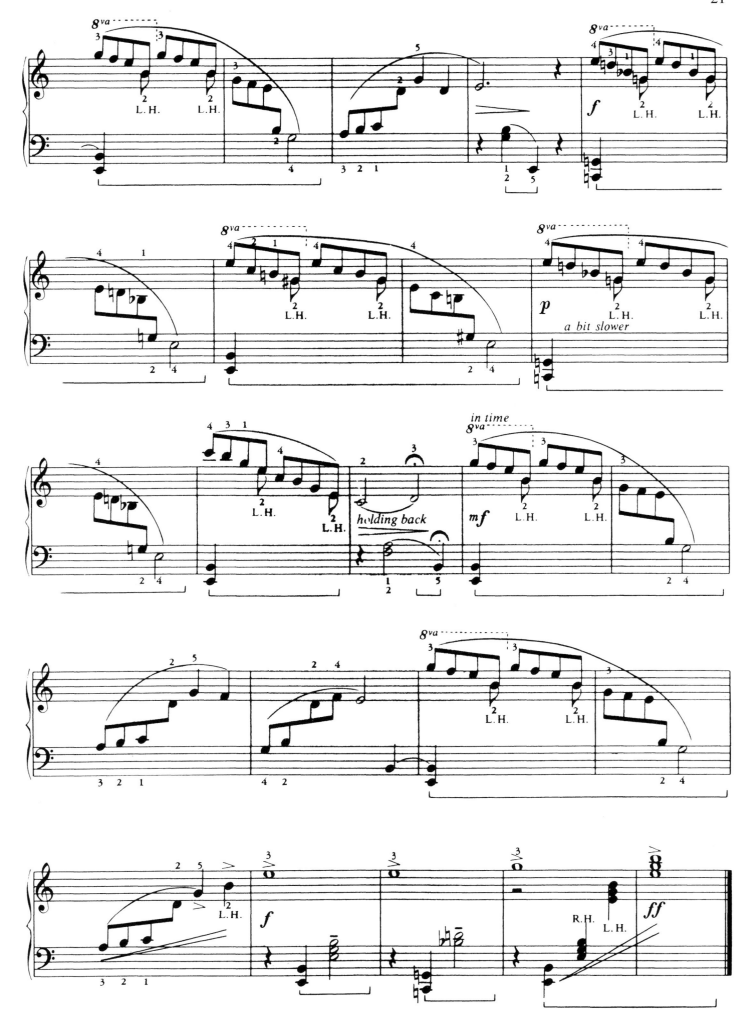

KEY OF E MINOR

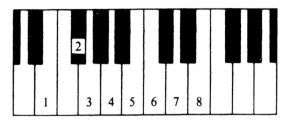

Write the names of the keys in the boxes

Here are the notes of the scale of E Minor in 4 octaves, the 7 chords of the scale and the authentic cadence. Write the key signature at the beginning of each staff, and fill in with pencil all of the notes that will be played on black keys.

The chords of the E Minor scale

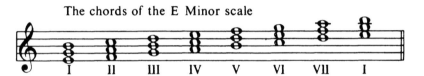

Authentic cadence in root position

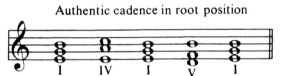

Practice the scale, chords and cadence as your teacher directs.

The following piece, ELFIN PRANKS, is written in the key of E Minor. Before you play it, write the key signature at the beginning of each staff.

ELFIN PRANKS

Soft pedal to the end

24

KEY OF B MAJOR

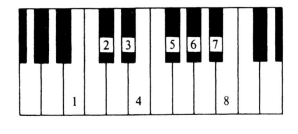

Write the names of the keys in the boxes

Here are the notes of the scale of B Major in 4 octaves, the 7 chords of the scale and the authentic cadence. Write the key signature at the beginning of each staff, and fill in with pencil all of the notes that will be played on black keys.

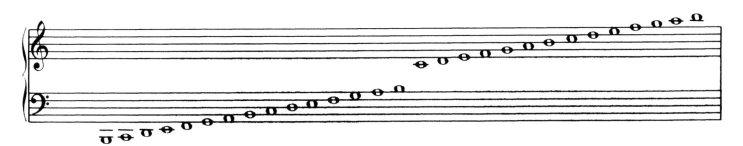

The chords of the B Major scale

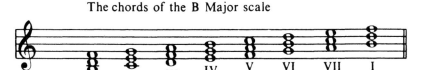

Authentic cadence in root position

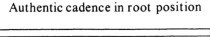

Practice the scale, chords and cadence as your teacher directs.

The following piece, ORIENTAL WIND CHIMES, is written in the key of B Major. Actually, only 5 tones of the scale are used in this piece. This type of scale is called Pentatonic, and it is associated with music of the Far East and with folk music. Write the key signature at the beginning of each staff.

ORIENTAL WIND CHIMES

Moderately

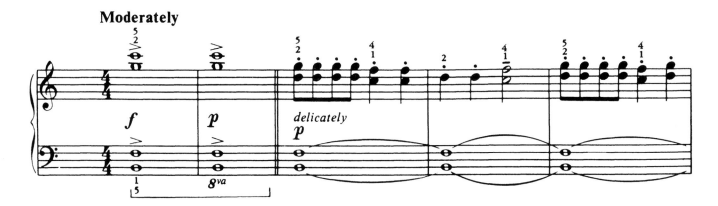

26

KEY OF B MINOR

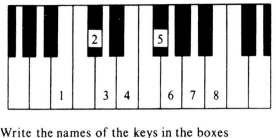

Write the names of the keys in the boxes

☐ ☐ ☐ ☐ ☐ ☐ ☐ ☐

Here are the notes of the scale of B Minor in 4 octaves, the 7 chords of the scale and the authentic cadence. Write the key signature at the beginning of each staff, and fill in with pencil all of the notes that will be played on black keys.

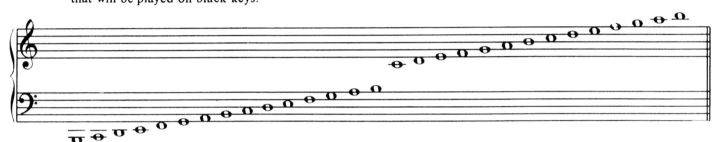

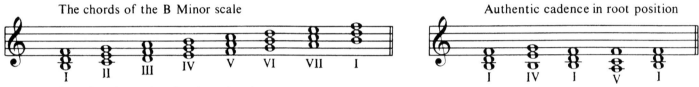

Practice the scale, chords and cadence as your teacher directs.

The following piece, THE DEEP BLUE SEA, is written in the key of B Minor. Before you play it, write the key signature at the beginning of each staff.

THE DEEP BLUE SEA

28

KEY OF F MAJOR

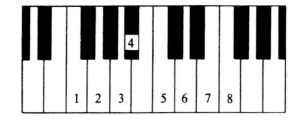

Write the names of the keys in the boxes

Here are the notes of the scale of F Major in 4 octaves, the 7 chords of the scale and the authentic cadence. Write the key signature at the beginning of each staff, and fill in with pencil all of the notes that will be played on black keys.

The chords of the F Major scale

I   II   III   IV   V   VI   VII   I

Authentic cadence in root position

I   IV   I   V   I

Practice the scale, chords and cadence as your teacher directs.

The following piece, SWISS MUSIC BOX, is written in the key of F Major. Before you play it, write the key signature at the beginning of each staff.

SWISS MUSIC BOX

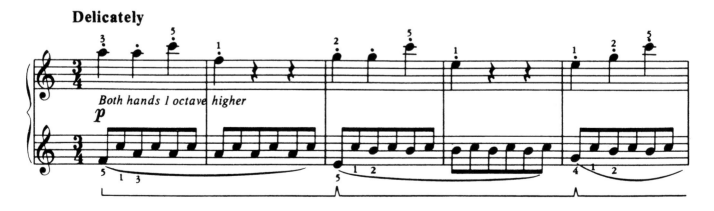

Delicately

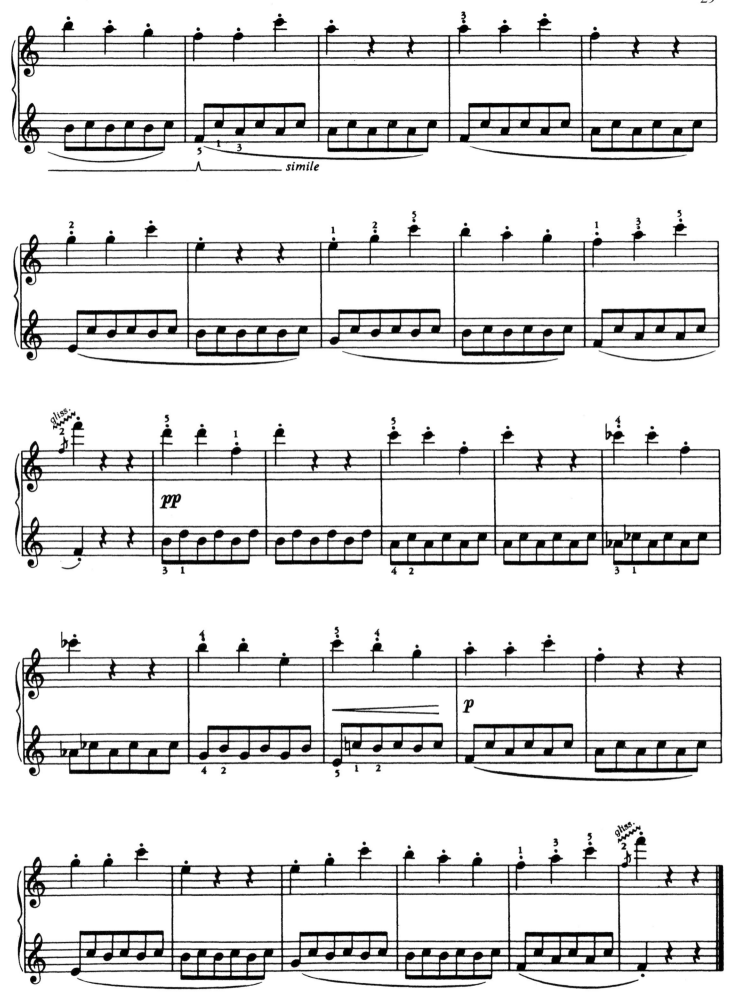

KEY OF F MINOR

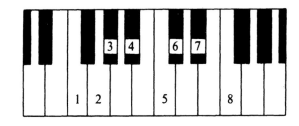

Write the names of the keys in the boxes

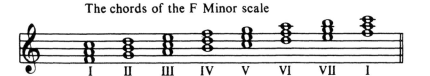

Here are the notes of the scale of F Minor in 4 octaves, the 7 chords of the scale and the authentic cadence. Write the key signature at the beginning of each staff, and fill in with pencil all of the notes that will be played on black keys.

The chords of the F Minor scale · · · · · · · · · · · · · Authentic cadence in root position

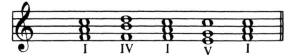 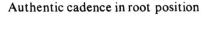

I II III IV V VI VII I · · · · · · · · · · · I IV I V I

Practice the scale, chords and cadence as your teacher directs.

The following piece, LAND OF PHAROAH, is written in the key of F Minor. Before you play it, write the key signature at the beginning of each staff.
Can you tell which tone of the Harmonic Minor scale has been additionally altered to create the Oriental Minor scale ?

LAND OF PHARAOH

With drowsy motion

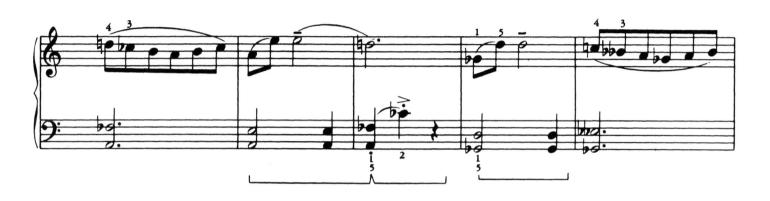

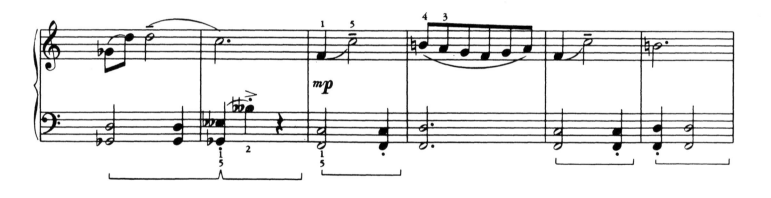

WILLIAM GILLOCK (1917–1993), noted music educator and composer of piano music, was born in LaRussell, Missouri, where he learned to play the piano at an early age. After graduating from Central Methodist College, his musical career led him to long tenures in New Orleans, Louisiana and Dallas, Texas, where he was always in great demand as a teacher, clinician, and composer. Called the "Schubert of children's composers" in tribute to his extraordinary melodic gift, Gillock composed numerous solos and ensembles for students of all levels. He was honored on multiple occasions by the National Federation of Music Clubs (NFMC) with the Award of Merit for Service to American Music, and his music continues to be remarkably popular throughout the United States and throughout the world.